THE NATIONAL
D-DAY MEMORIAL

Evolution of an Idea

BYRON DICKSON, ARCHITECT

BADGE OF SHAEF

This badge graphically identified
the Supreme Headquarters Allied
Expeditionary Force (abbreviated
SHAEF and pronounced "shafe.")
SHAEF, formed in Teddington,
London in December 1943, was
the base of operations for the
Commander of the Allied Forces
in northwest Europe until July 1945.
U.S. Gen. Dwight D. Eisenhower
was in command of SHAEF
throughout its existence.

THE NATIONAL
D-DAY MEMORIAL
Evolution of an Idea

The story of the development of a national tribute to all servicemen
and women involved in the Normandy invasion June 6, 1944.

Printing and binding: Bison Printing, Bedford, Virginia

ISBN: 978-0-615-44142-9

Byron Dickson is president of Dickson Architects & Associates of
Roanoke, VA. An alumnus of The University of Virginia School of
Architecture, he served in the armed forces during the Vietnam conflict.
That experience, combined with his career and love of history, led him
to help lay the groundwork to eventually design and build the National
D-Day Memorial located in nearby Bedford, VA. Dickson Architects
& Associates was established in 1971, and has practiced continually in
Virginia and neighboring states.

Edwina Dickson, office manager for Dickson & Associates, served as
the photography editor for images contained in this book.

Garnette Helvey Bane, of Garnette Bane & Associates, LLC, Editor
and publicist.

Liz Frankl and **Ananda Young** of Frankl Creative Group, Inc.,
Book design and layout.

Cover: The Overlord Arch at The National D-Day Memorial
Photography Credits: National Archives and Dickson Architects
Title Page: Final Tribute under the Overlord Arch at The National D-Day Memorial

American colors fly in Flag Circle along with the other eleven nations who participated in the D Day invasion.

CONTENTS

Acknowledgements

A special thanks to everyone who made the D-Day Memorial and this book possible.

My wife Edwina, who tirelessly edited and filed over two thousand images.

My editor Garnette Helvey Bane, who pulled it all together.

Liz Frankl and Ananda Young, who provided graphic expertise.

J. Robert Slaughter, the "Godfather" of the Memorial, who never gave up the dream during the eleven years of trying times during project development.

Gen. William B. Rossen, who provided endless inspiration, and possessed a keen sense of scale and proportion.

Richard Burrow, who served as president of the Memorial Foundation during the design and construction phases.

Bonnie Carver, who served as the architect's in-house project manager, and on-site representative.

Frank Caldwell and **Proctor Harvey**, both professionals, who assisted with great passion in the civil engineering and landscape architecture, respectively.

The Hon. Mike Shelton, Mayor of Bedford, who was instrumental in securing the Memorial for the City of Bedford.

The Hon. Lucile Boggess, member of the Bedford County Board of Supervisors, whose two brothers were killed during the D-Day invasion, and who tirelessly supported the efforts of Mayor Shelton.

Paul Dorrell, Director of Leopold International Gallery, who assembled the sculptural artists.

Jim Brothers, who brought the Memorial to life with his inspiring sculpture.

Matt Kirby, who crafted *Final Tribute*.

Jimmy Windle, Project Manager, who coordinated all site construction during Phases Two and Three.

Vaughn Tomblin, Project Superintendent, who supervised all site activities during Phases Two and Three, and never encountered a problem he couldn't solve.

Terry Dobyns, **Cliff Coleman** and the many construction entrepreneurs, who guided their companies through the delivery process.

Kip Connelly, who provided wise counsel and constant encouragement.

All of the Foundation Board Members over the years, who gave freely of their time to see the Memorial become a reality.

All of the workers, tradesmen and **craftspeople** who provided their labor and talent in pursuit of a world-class commemorative.

The many veterans, D-Day and otherwise, who have supported the Memorial through the vagaries of creation, we all want to say a very special, "Thank You."

EDITOR'S NOTE: *The time frame of this book begins in the early 1990s, when Dickson Architects began providing services to the original D-Day Memorial Committee, and ends with the formal dedication on June 6, 2001. Certain improvements that were either "on the drawing board," or in the process of being fabricated, are included. Beyond the window of this book are alterations and additions to the Memorial, initiated by others, and not the work of Dickson Architects.*

A Final Tribute

...to the Valor, Fidelity, and Sacrifice of the Allied Forces on D-Day

6 JUNE 1944

D-DAY — JUNE 6, 1944

"About 150 yards from shore – despite the warning from someone behind me to 'Keep your head down!' – I cautiously peeped up. I could see that the craft about twenty-five yards to our right and a couple hundred yards ahead, were targeted by small arms. Fiery tracer bullets skipped and bounced off the ramp and sides as they zeroed in before the ramps fell. I said to anyone close enough to hear above the bedlam: 'Men, we're going to catch hell. Be ready!'"

– Bob Slaughter, U.S. Army Sgt.
29th Infantry Division, 116th Infantry Regiment, D Company

Author of *Omaha Beach and Beyond*

A formation of B-26 Marauders approaches the French Coast.

CHAPTER ONE

Invasion

On a June morning in 1944, a damp chill filled the air as dawn broke along a 50-mile stretch of the Northern French coast. More than 160,000 troops comprising the Allied Expeditionary Forces waited nervously for the signal to forge ahead into the "jaws of hell." Forever remembered as D-Day, the invasion signaled the long-awaited breach of fortress Europe, which had been dubbed by Supreme Allied Commander, U.S. Gen. Dwight D. Eisenhower, as the "Great Crusade."

The Normandy shoreline, scene of the battle, was divided into five zones: Gold, Juno, and Sword, where the British and Canadians landed; and Utah and Omaha Beaches, where the Americans came ashore. In addition to land operations, more than 5,000 ships and 13,000 aircraft participated in the bloody campaign. More than 1,000 transport aircraft delivered American, British, and Canadian troops behind enemy lines in the pre-dawn darkness. In the end, D-Day, the Allies' invasion on June 6, 1944, was the largest amphibious assault in history – one that dramatically changed the course of World War II in the European Theater.

The allied Forces were comprised of combat and support units from the United States, Australia, Belgium, Canada, Czechoslovakia, France, Greece, the Netherlands, New Zealand, Norway, Poland, and the United Kingdom.

In early 1944, 750,000 American troops trained in England. By invasion time, the number of Allies participating had doubled. Prior to the invasion, American and British units conducted multiple joint training exercises for months in preparation for the scheduled engagement.

For a week prior to crossing the English Channel, troops boarded ships destined for the Normandy coast. The weather at the time of the scheduled invasion was miserable, and sufficiently severe as to postpone the attack for a day. When the weather broke, Gen. Eisenhower issued the attack command for Tuesday, June 6.

Early on D-Day the air and sea bombardment began. H-hour for the landing forces was scheduled for 6:30 a.m., and continued along all zones for the following 90 minutes.

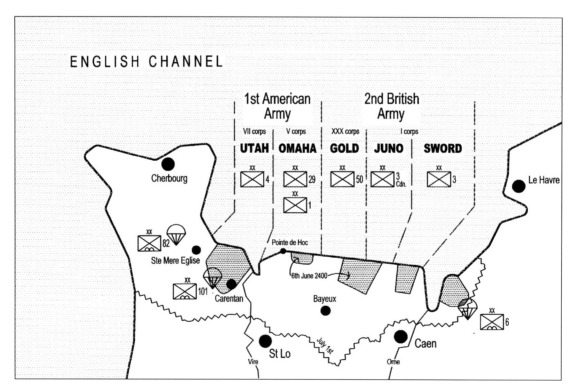

6 June 1944 – D-Day Invasion – Normandy, France.

Throughout the day they came.

Shortly after midnight, three airborne divisions departed for inland objectives on the east and west flanks of the invasion zones. Approximately an hour before the landing commenced, American Rangers began their ascent of the cliffs at Pointe du Hoc, their objective to take out German gun emplacements overlooking the western landing zones.

Of the two American zones, Omaha Beach was the most difficult. Sea and air bombardments did not prove to be as damaging to the German shore defenses as originally thought. For much of the morning, soldiers from the 1st and 29th Divisions were pinned down by unmerciful gunfire coming from the cliffs high above the beach. Because of the soldiers' bravery and resourcefulness, a foothold was established by evening. In the following days, both divisions moved out to take their objectives, including the coastal village of Isigny.

The 4th-Division operations went smoothly on Utah Beach, thanks to landing 2,000 yards south of their intended mark where defenses were strong. By mid-morning, the beachhead was secured, and troops moved inland to make contact with the airborne divisions scattered throughout the area.

Massive numbers of troops and material poured across the English Channel during the invasion and for days afterwards.

Soldiers climbed up the cliffs to capture the high ground.

The regular British Infantry landed on Sword Beach without serious casualties and by the end of the day had penetrated several miles into enemy territory. On Juno Beach, the Canadians suffered the second highest percentage of casualties among the five beachheads. On Gold Beach, casualties were also significant; however, the British managed to reach the outskirts of Bayeux by nightfall.

> *"Casualties were high, reaching close to 10,000. Omaha and Utah Beaches suffered upwards of 5,000 and 200 respectively."*

While not all objectives were met initially, the conclusion of the battle found the Allies permanently established in northern Europe. Hitler's formidable "Atlantic Wall" had been breached.

Casualties were high, reaching close to 10,000. Omaha and Utah Beaches suffered upwards of 5,000 and 200 respectively. American airborne casualties totaled 2,500. German Field Marshal Irwin Rommel, who commanded the defense of the northwestern French coast, reported significant enemy losses during the D-Day invasion with estimates in excess of 5,000.

Above: Gen. Eisenhower talks with departing airborne troops prior to their nighttime drop into enemy territory.

Left: The world hears of the successful invasion that has come to be known as D-Day.

Normandy Today

Clockwise from top left: Colleville Cemetery in Normandy is the final resting place for many of the soldiers not returning home.

A lone landing craft serves as a subtle reminder of past events that led to the downfall of Hitler's Third Reich.

The serenity of Omaha Beach belies the fierce combat that took place there in June 1944.

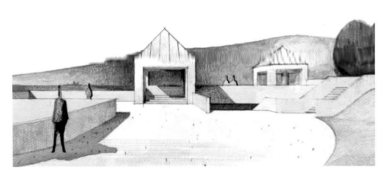

Above: Aerial view of the
original Memorial study for
Mill Mountain in Roanoke, VA

Left: View from the roof-top
promenade overlooking
The Roanoke Valley

CHAPTER TWO

Location

The men behind the D-Day Memorial movement shared a painful history dating back to 1944. Years later, on a late spring day in 1987, they happened to gather for a backyard barbecue. Long before this casual evening event, they had fought together in battle – and survived to tell about their experiences. They were D-Day veterans, proud of their combat ordeal during the Allied invasion along the Normandy coast. During this spring outing they pledged their efforts in pursuit of a future goal: to recognize those soldiers who fought, were wounded, or died in one of the bloodiest battles in modern history. Little did they know at the time, just how momentous this commitment to a permanent commemorative would become.

ROANOKE

In July 1989, Dickson Architects, a Roanoke design firm, was brought on board to assist in the planning and design of a memorial to recognize D-Day as the largest invasion in history.

The committee first sought to locate their project atop Mill Mountain within the City of Roanoke. The early days were difficult due to little funding and limited promotion. It wasn't long until the project met with opposition from various interests who also wanted to locate on the mountain. The committee soon lost interest and moved on.

At Roanoke's invitation, emphasis shifted to another site within the city. This location was identified as Gateway Fountain and positioned in the Gainsboro redevelopment area. Gateway offered the opportunity to develop a linear park connecting downtown with the Roanoke Civic Center. The development would involve the abandoned Norfolk Southern train station, which would serve as an education center. Unfortunately, issues involving traffic flow and acquisition of additional land surfaced. These limitations would have seriously curtailed development and, ultimately, caused this location to be abandoned also.

Right: Vacant train station that was to become the Education Center.

Below: Gateway Fountain site plan

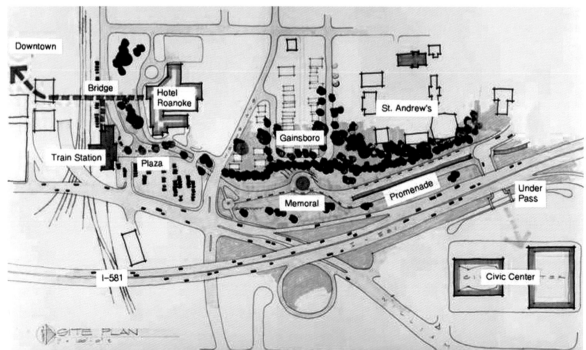

Bedford

In late summer of 1994, after learning of the obstacles being encountered in the Roanoke Valley; leaders from Bedford, Virginia, stepped forward with an invitation to locate the Memorial in their community. Several sites in the Bedford area were offered for consideration. The preferred site was next to Bedford Elementary School and afforded a splendid view of the surrounding areas from the hilltop location. Convenient access was available from an adjacent major thoroughfare, U.S. Route 460 connecting the state east and west.

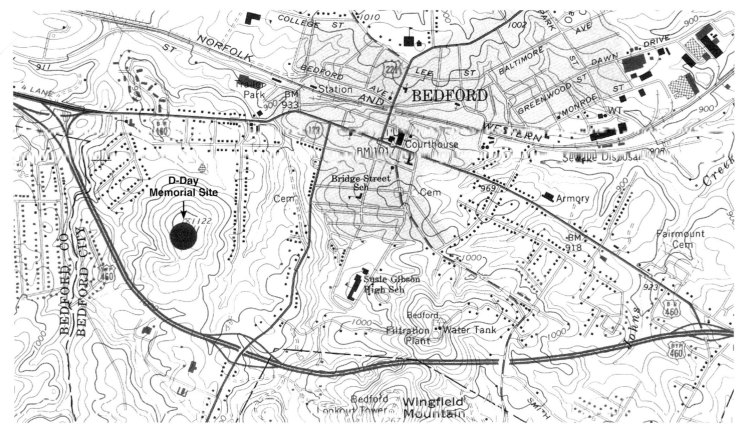

Map of Bedford, VA showing the location of The National D-Day Memorial.

On Veterans Day, November 11, 1994, the D-Day Memorial Foundation formally announced it would be moving to Bedford. The site posed no serious limitations on program objectives. When completed, the Memorial would stand as a fitting tribute to all D-Day veterans, including the young soldiers from Bedford, who were among the first to assault the beaches of Normandy that June day in 1944. Their losses being so great as to bestow upon this small community, the dubious honor of losing more sons per capita than any other city or town in America during World War II – a total of 22 during the invasion window.

Site Analysis and Planning

Immediately after announcing plans to go to Bedford, intense site analysis would begin. Site assets, fundamental to success were numerous; including location, access, ambiance, and community backing. Over the four years during the Roanoke experience, the design program had evolved into a sophisticated set of goals for commemorating the event and educating visitors about the D-Day invasion.

Aerial view of the Bedford site looking northwest.

Today, the completed D-Day Memorial occupies a position high on a hill inside Bedford's city limits. Circumferential views are unobstructed in all directions with the beautiful Blue Ridge Mountains and Peaks of Otter framing the northern skyline approximately ten miles away. The site overlooks Bedford's small downtown central business district where church spires tower majestically above the charming old-town structures. The size, topography and panorama of the site make it the ideal location for the D-Day Memorial.

In order to construct the Memorial, an entry road approximately a half-mile long was required to access the hilltop, where the primary commemorative would be located. The crown of the hill was close to a perfect spherical shape, resembling the top of a basketball. This geometry provided for the development of a circular drive with the commemorative positioned within the perimeter roadway. The Education Center was planned for the brow of the hill, just below the pinnacle. It would be the first component to be reached as visitors proceeded up the access roadway.

All elements of the D-Day Memorial complex fell comfortably into place, giving ease of approach to vehicular traffic, providing ample parking within convenient walking distance, and allowing those with restricted mobility unobstructed access to all features.

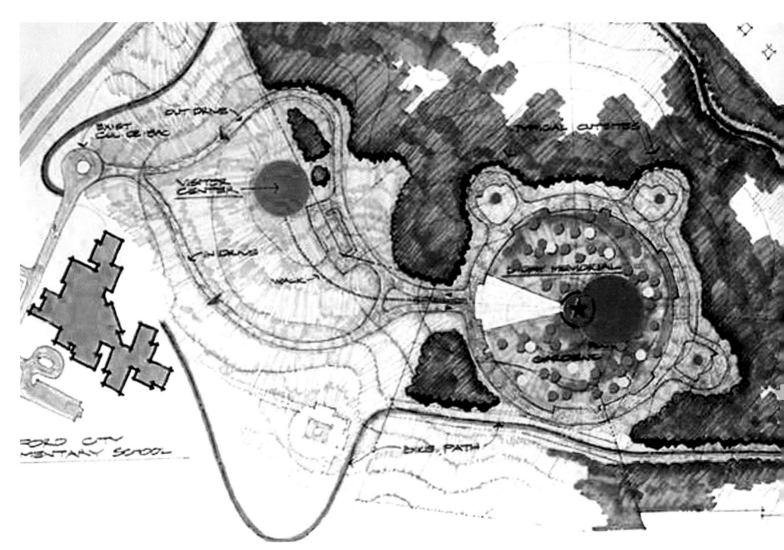

Original Bedford site plan showing access from the elementary school cul-de-sac.

CEREMONIAL GROUND BREAKING

November 11, 1997

From top: The view from the Education Center site looking up toward the eventual location of Victory Plaza and Overlord Arch.

Ground Breaking was a great day for the Foundation, the design team, and the community.

The view looking northeast toward the Bedford community.

"Finally, we're moving dirt, it's exciting after all these years."

— Byron Dickson, Architect

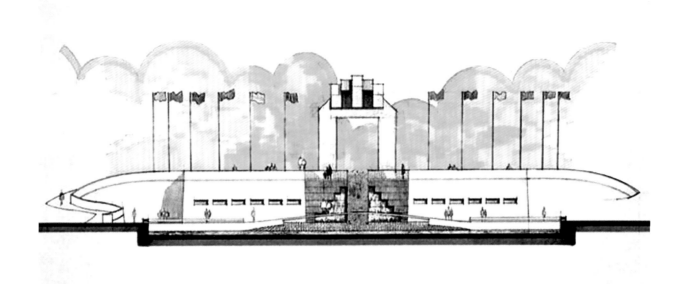

An early design study

CHAPTER THREE

Design

Two unsuccessful attempts in Roanoke gave the D-Day Memorial Committee, later to be known as the D-Day Memorial Foundation, an opportunity to fine tune its program requirements. The Roanoke experience also pointed out the importance of proper site selection in developing the full potential of the Memorial. The Bedford site was fully capable of maximizing the program goals, which included commemorating the event, educating future generations, and stimulating the interest of all visitors across a wide range of ages and backgrounds.

THE PARKING DILEMMA

To assure the Memorial's success in accommodating visitors, it was imperative to have convenient access and proximity to the hilltop. With the strong circular influence imposed by existing topography, an appropriate strategy was needed. There was no area on the site to conveniently locate a traditional rectilinear parking area. To solve this problem, it was decided to position parking along the perimeter of the circular outer roadway. This concept would place all parking stalls in close proximity to the Memorial environs, giving visitors entry to the grounds via five entry points or gates positioned equally around the circular drive.

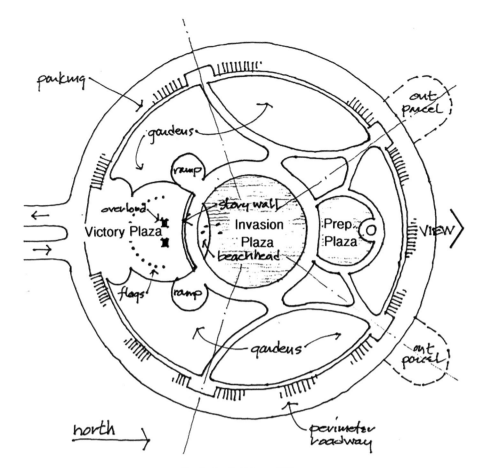

Initial Site Plan

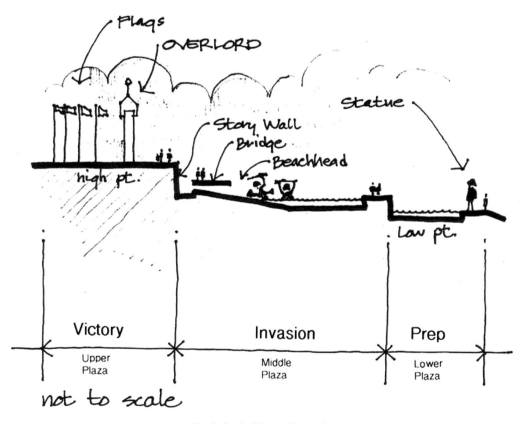

Initial Site Section

THE CONCEPT

The Foundation wanted the Memorial to identify and give meaning to three important aspects of the overall invasion experience. First were the years spent in England preparing for the assault on the northern French coast; second, was the actual landing of the amphibious craft; and third, was the victory over the intense coastal defenses built by the German forces. To properly recognize these three phases, it was concluded that each should be assigned a plaza within the perimeter vehicular drive.

VICTORY PLAZA

Victory Plaza, the highest elevation on the hilltop, would celebrate the successful outcome of the invasion. The featured commemorative, *Overload Arch*, is positioned at the center of *Victory Plaza*.

At the outer perimeter of *Victory Plaza*, will be positioned the flags of each of the 12 nations that participated in the invasion. Located on the plaza's minor axis will be two shelters emulating the traditional field tents of that period. Two large circular ramps, connecting at each shelter, will direct visitors from *Victory Plaza* to *Invasion Plaza* on the next level down from the hilltop.

The plan for Victory Plaza

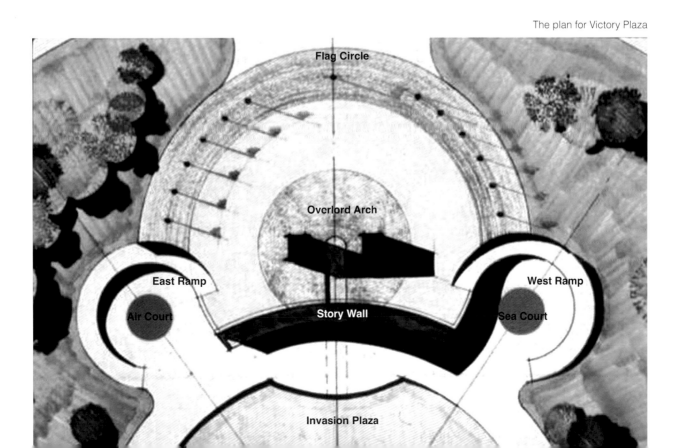

Left: A Flag Circle study

Below: Sketch of the Flag Circle looking east.

OVERLORD ARCH

At the center of *Victory Plaza* would be constructed the featured commemorative, the iconic *Overload Arch*. The Memorial Foundation stressed the importance that *Overlord Arch* have recognizable features relating to the D-Day event. Any abstract interpretive form was rejected. In response to the Foundation's concern, it was decided that the design would consider three important aspects of the event – WHERE, WHAT and WHEN.

WHERE

The scene of the battle was northern Europe. Throughout the continent's history, many nations used the classical arch form to celebrate victory over their adversaries. One significant example of this motif is the Arch of Titus, built in Rome to commemorate the Emperor's military exploits during the first century A.D. The arch was chosen as the basic form for the D-Day commemorative.

The Arch of Titus

WHAT

D-Day's two most enduring symbols during the war were the black-and-white stripes used to identify Allied aircraft, and the invasion's code name, OVERLORD. It was decided that the arch 'attic' would use alternating black-and-white granite stones and beneath the attic would be inscribed the code name OVERLORD.

Identification bands

Code name

WHEN

The prevailing architecture of the day was a style known as Art Deco, a design mode distinguished by clean shapes, soft edges, and reflective surfaces. The streamlined appearance of the polished granite reflects this fanciful style.

Surrounding the base of *Overlord Arch* is a granite ring with the inscribed names of the five landing zones: Utah, Omaha, Gold, Juno, and Sword. Immediately below the Arch is the dedicatory inscription:

In Tribute to the Valor, Fidelity and Sacrifice
of the Allied Forces on D-Day
6 June 1944

Adjacent to the above dedicatory inscription is a somber sculptural piece by Matt Kirby entitled *Final Tribute*. This piece will be discussed in further detail later in this chapter.

Arch Statistics

Height: 44'-6"

Width: 38'-0"

Depth: 8'-4"

Opening: 20'-0" x 24'-8" high

Total granite pieces: 94

Total granite surface: 2,977 sq. ft.

Total granite weight: 366 tons

Concrete frame: 562 tons

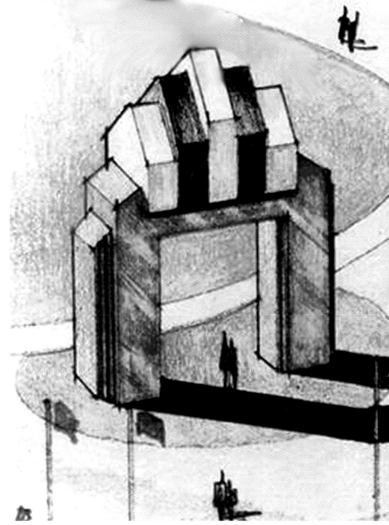

Early arch rendering

From *Victory Plaza* to the north, visitors will look out over *Invasion Plaza*. To protect them from falling into the collection pool below, a special railing design would be imported from the Colleville Cemetery in Normandy and used with the American Battle Monuments Commission's permission. It is fitting that this cemetery, where so many D-Day battle casualties rest to this day, share a common design element with The National D-Day Memorial.

Moving in the opposite direction toward the south, visitors will enjoy a walk down a landscaped promenade paved with cobblestones leading to the Garrison Flag. It is planned that this walk will lead to the future Education Center at the brow of the hill overlooking the elementary school.

INVASION PLAZA

A casual stroll down either of the large ramps will lead visitors from the upper *Victory Plaza* to the large assembly area below – given the name *Invasion Plaza*. It is here that a sense of the intense combat that took place that morning in June 1944, will be keenly felt.

Generally, the plaza is circular with two courtyards attached; the *Air Court* to the east, and the *Sea Court* to the west. *Invasion Plaza* is separated from the above *Victory Plaza* by a 20-foot high *Storywall*. A bridge, crossing the *Beachhead Diorama*, will connect the two courts and allow visitors to get up close and personal with the sculptural works of artist Jim Brothers.

At the north end of *Invasion Plaza*, is another overlook and two sets of classical stairs leading to the sedate *English Garden*, a typically British construct.

Above: Early study of Storywall and Beachhead Diorama

Opposite: Final rendering of Overlord Arch

MODEL VIEWS

From top: Beachhead Diorama showing Invasion Pool, Beach, and crossing bridge.

South end of Invasion Plaza shows Storywall and Beachhead Diorama.

View of Beachhead Diorama facing Storywall and Victory Plaza.

LARGE ASSEMBLY AREA

At the center of *Invasion Plaza* will be a large paved area set aside primarily for gatherings, both private and public. Containing 50,000 square feet of assembly area, the enclosure is ideal for concerts and anniversary celebrations. Quite often, temporary seating will be provided, which gives the plaza a capacity of over 3,000 guests.

Access to *Invasion Plaza* is from each side, being fed from both ramps (down from *Victory Plaza*) and four entry gates positioned adjacent to the perimeter parking. Also, access up from the *English Garden* will be provided via the *Classical Stairs*.

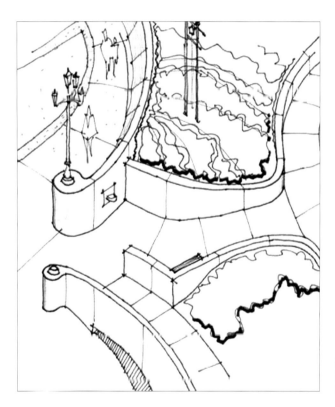

Side access to
Invasion Plaza from
ramps and entry gate

STORYWALL

Storywall describes the struggle to take the high ground above the beaches of Normandy. To illustrate this effort, a 20-foot high sculpture created by artist Jim Brothers, will occupy a position at the centerline focal point. Adjacent to Jim's piece on each side are two cascading water features emphasizing the vertical movement of the soldiers *Scaling the Wall*, as the sculpture will be named. Water will be collected at the base of this focal point and flow gently under the bridge and across the beach.

BEACHHEAD DIORAMA

The *Beachhead Diorama* will feature the viewing bridge, beach scene, invasion pool, and landing craft.

The viewing bridge will connect each side of the Plaza and will allow visitors to get a close-up look at the *Storywall* and *Diorama*. It will provide a marvelous view upward of *Overlord Arch* and in the opposite direction, a head-on look directly into the landing craft. It is an excellent point from which to view the entire *Invasion Plaza*.

The simulated beach scene will consist of an exposed aggregate concrete with two of Jim Brothers' sculptures, *Across the Beach* and *Death on the Shore*, placed appropriately with the latter partially submerged in the pool.

From left: Model of viewing bridge; Model of beach scene

It is planned that the *Invasion Pool* be a unique feature and that it have animation. The original fountain spray heads will be adjusted to simulate the impact of enemy gunfire and will be set to randomly explode. Placed throughout the pool will be obstacles called "hedgehogs," together with another of Jim Brothers' sculptures entitled *Through the Surf* revealing the tortuous trek to reach the beach.

Across from the viewing bridge will be a stylized "Higgins Boat," or "Landing Craft, Personnel – Large" (LCPL) constructed of granite and configured in debarkation profile.

AIR AND SEA COURTS

These courtyards will be defined by the circular ramps connecting *Invasion Plaza* with *Victory Plaza* above. Each shall be dedicated to honoring air and sea (operation Neptune) activity during the invasion.

Sea Courts study model

NECROLOGY WALLS

Surrounding *Invasion Plaza* will be the Necrology Walls, memorializing the names of the fallen on D-Day. The east Necrology Wall contains the names of soldiers from allied nations. The west Necrology Wall will contain the names of American soldiers.

Necrology wall study model

CLASSICAL STAIRS

Leading down toward the *English Garden*, the *Classical Stairs* provide a transition from the architecture of war to the more serene traditional environment of Great Britain.

Classical Stairs sketch

From top: Invasion Plaza study model

Invasion Pool view

English Garden

Descending the *Classical Stairs* into the *English Garden*, the mood softens. Originally, the *English Garden* was envisioned to be the preparation plaza. Further study revealed the massive training and operational planning that took place during the two years prior to the invasion.

It was decided that the Garden would be a place for contemplation. Benches will be positioned along the walks, and landscaping will enhance the surroundings.

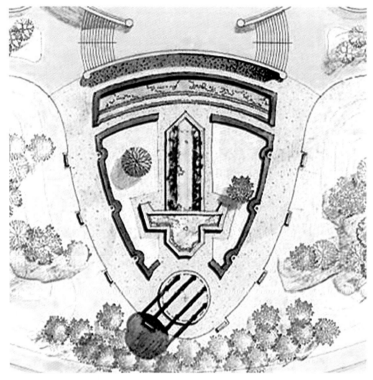

English Garden Plan

Originally conceived as a circular space (similar to *Invasion* and *Victory Plazas* above), the plan shape would evolve into a composition emulating the badge of Supreme Head-quarters Allied Expeditionary Force (SHAEF). This iconic badge was casually referred to as the "flaming sword," or Eisenhower Shoulder patch.

At the far end (north) of the Garden would be positioned The Eisenhower Gazebo in which would be placed Jim Brothers' statue of Gen. Dwight D. Eisenhower, Supreme Allied Commander. Along the walks at each side of the Garden, a bust of each member of the SHAEF general staff will be placed, three on each side. The Commanders were:

Air Chief Marshal Arthur Tedder, Deputy Supreme Allied Commander
Field Marshal Bernard Law Montgomery, 21st Army Group
Lt. Gen. Omar N. Bradley, 12th Army Group
Air Marshal Trafford Leigh-Mallory, Air Forces Commander
Adm. Bertram Ramsay, Naval Forces Commander
Lt. Gen. Bedell Smith, Chief of Staff

EISENHOWER GAZEBO

The primary feature of the *English Garden* is the *Eisenhower Gazebo*. The gazebo, or as some may refer to as a rotunda, is typical of the classical 'folly' found in 18th-Century gardens throughout England. The *Eisenhower Gazebo*, constructed of precast concrete, will employ the Tuscan architectural style.

Eisenhower Gazebo section study

Plaque wall elevation study

PLAQUE WALL

Opposite the *Eisenhower Gazebo*, and separating the *English Garden* from the higher *Invasion Plaza*, will be a wall supporting the *Classical Stairs*. On this wall, a three-section bronze plaque will be placed displaying Gen. Eisenhower's message to all assault troops on the morning of the invasion.

SCULPTURE

In 1997, Paul Dorrell, owner and director of the Leopold Gallery in Kansas City, MO, was selected by the Foundation to serve as consultant for matters related to sculptural aspects of the project. Soon after his appointment two sculptors were recommended: Jim Brothers (Lawrence, Kansas) and Matt Kirby (Baldwin City, Kansas) for creation of seven initial bronze pieces. Additional pieces would be considered when funding becomes available. The following pieces were either commissioned, or under consideration during the course of the project.

FINAL TRIBUTE

This traditional symbol of commemoration was taken from photographs of temporary wartime grave sites marked with a helmet on a rifle with "dog tags" attached. Matt Kirby was the lead sculptor on this first piece.

Field grave

Architect's sketch

Final Tribute

ACROSS THE BEACH

The second piece commissioned, and the first to show actual soldiers in combat, would become the sculptural icon of the Memorial. It was originally scheduled to be the focal point on the *Invasion Plaza* Beach; however, it would temporarily be located at the main entrance to *Victory Plaza* during construction of *Invasion Plaza*. Later it will be moved to the *Invasion Plaza* beach as originally planned. (The Foundation liked the piece in its temporary position and decided to move it back after a second piece was designed and cast to take its place on the beach.) Jim Brothers was the artist for each piece.

Valor, Fidelity, and Sacrifice

This became the new designation for *Across the Beach* after it was permanently relocated to the entrance planter at *Victory Plaza*.

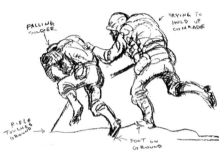

Architect's mock-up

Sculptor's sketch

Sculptor's clay

Scaling the Wall

The struggle to capture the high ground was depicted in this original piece by Jim Brothers. The underlying theme was taken from the heroic assault on Pointe de Hoc by the 2nd Ranger Battalion prior to the beachhead landings on Utah and Omaha. It will be the largest piece at the Memorial and measures nineteen feet tall. Four soldiers will be depicted as they climb their way to the top of the wall while enduring brutal enemy fire.

Architect's mock-up

Sculptor's sketch

Bronze soldiers

Through the Surf

Totally in the water *(Invasion Pool)*, this piece seeks to depict a soldier working his way through the surf trying to reach the beach. It will be viewed in the midst of strafing gun fire made real by the exploding water throughout the pool. Jim Brothers was selected as the artist for this piece.

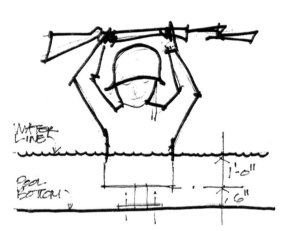

Architect's concept sketch

Invasion pool

Death on the Shore

As a poignant reminder of the sacrifice so many soldiers made that morning, this piece will show a fallen warrior at water's edge. There are many nuances to this piece, including the Bible which tumbled out of the infantryman's backpack. Jim Brothers was the selected artist for this piece.

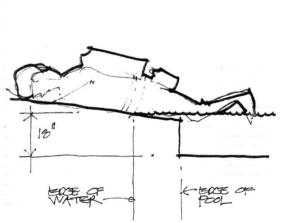

Architect's concept sketch

Beachhead

BEACH OBSTACLES

While somewhat of a utilitarian piece, the "hedgehogs" were deemed to possess certain artistic qualities that required them to be fabricated under the direction of the Memorial's lead sculptor, Jim Brothers.

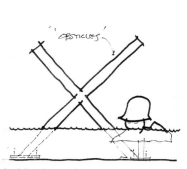
Architect's sketch

Architect's mock-up

Invasion pool

THE SUPREME COMMANDER

Inside the Gazebo is a replica by Jim Brothers of his statue of Gen. Dwight D. Eisenhower, Supreme Allied Commander, that today stands in the rotunda of the U.S. Capitol.

Sculptor's clay

Eisenhower Gazebo

THE LADY OF TREVIERES *(Le Monument aux Morts)*

In May 1921, a sculptural work by Edmond de Laheurie was unveiled in Trevieres, France, to commemorate the loss of 44 men from that town who died in World War I. In June of 1944, during the D-Day invasion, a shell struck the statue, tearing off a portion of the "Lady's" face.

During a visit to Normandy in the fall of 1998, Memorial architect Byron Dickson and lead sculptor Jim Brothers came upon this significant piece of art in the Trevieres town square. They were so impressed with her austere beauty and tenacity that they wanted to bring her back to Bedford. Not unexpectedly, the people of Trevieres did not want to part with their "Lady," but did agree to allow a casting to be made from the original statue.

With the help of Guy Wildenstein and French officials, this "carbon copy" of the wounded "Lady" was brought to Bedford and unveiled late in 2002.

This piece is a fitting tribute to the shared sacrifice between the U.S. and France, and to the cooperation between countries in putting together the effort required to give this second "Lady" a home at the Memorial.

The original Lady of Trevieres

The second "Lady" at the Memorial

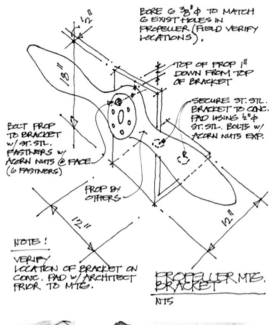

BORE 6 ⅜" Ø TO MATCH
6 EXIST HOLES IN
PROPELLER (FIELD VERIFY
LOCATIONS).

TOP OF PROP 1"
DOWN FROM TOP
OF BRACKET

SECURE ST. STL.
BRACKET TO CONC.
PAD USING ½" Ø
ST. STL. BOLTS W/
ACORN NUTS EXP.

BOLT PROP
TO BRACKET
W/ ST. STL.
FASTNRS W/
ACORN NUTS @ FACE
(6 FASTNRS)

PROP BY
OTHERS

NOTE!
VERIFY
LOCATION OF BRACKET ON
CONC. PAD W/ ARCHITECT
PRIOR TO MTG.

PROPELLER MTG.
BRACKET
NTS

From the Architect's Sketchbook

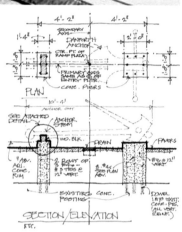

PLAN

SECTION/ELEVATION
NTS.

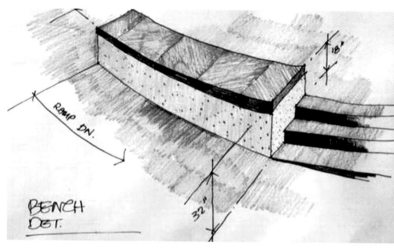

BENCH DET.

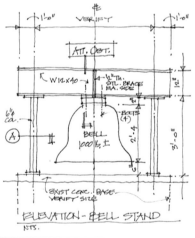

VERIFY

ATT. DET.

BELL
1000 ℔ ±

ELEVATION - BELL STAND
NTS.

...A DEEP MUTUAL RESPECT FOR THE TALENTS OF EACH...

Architect Dickson (left)
and Lead Sculptor Brothers

Early days of excavation work

CHAPTER FOUR

Build

Fund raising was an ongoing challenge. Because of this, the work had to be staged to coincide with available private and public support. The current level of giving governed the speed at which work progressed. Each step toward final completion required special design and construction skills. The Memorial needed five phases to be totally operational; three of which would be completed in approximately six years; two would remain unfinished at the time of dedication.

PHASE ONE –   **Site Preparation**
PHASE TWO –   **Victory Plaza**
PHASE THREE   **Invasion Plaza and English Garden**
PHASE FOUR –   **Education Center**
PHASE FIVE –   **Miscellaneous Improvements**

More rock than expected

Hilltop taking shape

At the conclusion of Phase One, the roadway was in place along with base paving, rough grading was complete, and underground utilities had been installed. In the above picture, the white structure is a tent that was used as a temporary assembly enclosure for special events during the period between completion of Phase One and the start of Phase Two. Temporary parking was now available on the hilltop.

Work was staged to accommodate the current level of giving, which varied greatly throughout the project. That factor prevented a fixed overall completion schedule and caused a delay between Phase One and Phase Two. On the other hand, Phase Three was started prior to completion of Phase Two. Unfortunately, Phase Four and Five have been delayed indefinitely.

PHASE ONE – SITE PREPARATION

Phase One got underway with an elaborate ground-breaking ceremony held on Veteran's Day, November 11, 1997. Virginia's governor, both state senators, members of the U.S. House of Representatives, and many local dignitaries attended the festivities.

Earlier in 1997, bids were received from interested contractors. The firm of Counts and Doybns, out of Rustburg, VA, was awarded the contract for Phase One. This work would include grading, utilities, and a temporary roadway, complete with base paving. Once completed, a wide range of VIPs would be given progress tours to let them know the D-Day Memorial was serious business. Among the visitors would be potential donors and members of the media, both essential to the construction effort if progress was to advance to the next phase.

At the conclusion of Phase One, members of the 29th Division erected a temporary memorial at the future site of Overlord Arch. Between two telephone poles was strung a banner with the motto of the 29th emblazoned thereon.

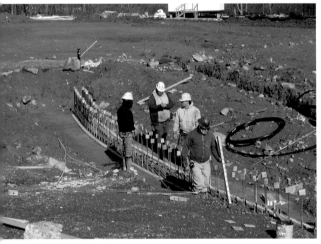

Clockwise from top:

Roadway preparation

Foundation steel rises

Footing excavation

Utility trenching

Footings being formed and cast

Phase Two – Victory Plaza

The bid for Phase Two was let on May 13, 1990. Five weeks later, the Foundation awarded a contract for the construction of *Victory Plaza* to Coleman-Adams, a Lynchburg, Virginia-based general contractor.

Victory Plaza includes *Overlord Arch*, *Flag Circle*, tent shelters, and *Storywall* (unfinished). Due to the weight of *Overlord Arch* and a sizable retaining wall, the foundation work was massive. The early activity necessitated the installation of large quantities of structurally sound reinforced concrete. Much of this work was completed during the winter months.

Skilled and dedicated formwork technicians worked in sometimes difficult conditions in order to put in place concrete work that required exacting tolerances. Their accuracy and finish quality are reflected in the precise location of the vertical and horizontal granite pieces that were to follow.

Foundation walls in place

Retaining wall below Overlord Arch

From top: Precise location of reinforcing steel was an important structural requirement.

Major retaining wall takes shape under Overlord Arch.

Storywall support structure in progress.

After completion of foundation work, focus shifted to above-grade work. With great anticipation the first stages of *Overlord Arch* construction commenced. First the formwork and reinforcing was accurately put in place.

Clockwise from top left: First leg starts up; First leg formed; Both legs formed; Formwork complete.

Once the forms were stripped and the concrete properly cured, application of the granite cladding began, after cladding is in place, the attic top stones were installed.

Clockwise from top left: Forms stripped and ready for granite; Granite starts up each leg; Cathedral stone being lifted; Capping out the attic.

PHASE THREE – INVASION PLAZA

Phase Three consists of *Invasion Plaza* and the *English Garden*. Installation of these elements marked the completion of the commemorative portion of the Memorial. Like Phase Two, this phase was completed by Coleman-Adams. This phase would receive the majority of the sculptural pieces. Memorial architect and lead sculptor, Jim Brothers worked closely to achieve the goals set forth by the Foundation.

The construction schedule was trimmed to nine months in order to allow Memorial dedication to occur on June 6, 2001, the 57th anniversary of the D-Day invasion. Work on Phase Three was scheduled to begin in August, 2000.

Above: One of the first items to be addressed in Phase Three was construction of the two ramps leading from Victory Plaza down to Invasion Plaza

Right: Each ramp required forming a highly articulated curved concrete wall that changes height and thickness over a vertical drop of 20 feet.

From the top: Low walls define Invasion Plaza.

Pouring concrete for the floor of Invasion Plaza.

Phase Three site work included final grading of all areas between the Plazas and the perimeter drive.

For the most part, *Invasion Plaza* was constructed of concrete low walls and flat work.

Invasion pool required the installation of concrete risers, an exposed aggregate beachhead, a stylized landing craft, and a raised bridge connecting the east and west sides of *Invasion Plaza*.

From Top: Beachhead exposed aggregate concrete being poured; Land craft concrete frame being poured.

From the top:
Surveying crew at work

Walks being fomed

Positioning the entry gate

Clockwise from top left:
Concrete finishing work

Bridge ready to receive railing

Waterfall inspection

This page: Invasion Plaza nears completion.

Above: Invasion Plaza prior to beginning work on the English Garden beyond.

Left: Polishing the Sea Court's Ship's Bell

From top:
The "Grasshopper" arrives.

Tibbs and Barksdale oversee
installation of the Aeronca L-3B.

Contractor assists
restoration crew in assembling
and securing aircraft.

AIR AND SEA COURTS

On each side of *Invasion Plaza*, opposite the *Storywall*, are two courts, one for air and the other for sea. The *Air Court* is particularly noteworthy, due to the efforts of a group of aviation enthusiasts at New London Airport. These folks, led by the intrepid Rucker Tibbs, restored an Aeronca L-3B "grasshopper," used for liaison and observation by Allied ground forces. The aircraft was donated by Morton Lester of Martinsville, Virginia. John Barksdale of Rustburg, Virginia orchestrated the restoration and donation. While this particular aircraft did not see action on D-Day, it is similar to other "grasshoppers" that were used during the assault on northern France in 1944. The L-3B will eventually be moved to the Education Center and be suspended from the ceiling in the grand lobby.

Aeronca L-3B "Grasshopper" is at home in Air Court.

Top right: Precast concrete classical balustrade being installed.

Top left: Granite stone caps are lowered into position.

Botton: Classical stair balustrade sits atop the separation wall between Invasion Plaza and English Garden.

ENGLISH GARDEN

The last major feature to be completed, the *English Garden* is well below the crown of the hill *(Overlord Arch)* and at the opposite end of the Memorial axis. Due to the lack of full funding, much of the *English Garden* was not completed until after the formal dedication.

Top: Sword planter taking shape.

Bottom: Completed planter with flowers provide colors found in the SHAEF badge.

Top to bottom:
Planter walls being installed
in the shape of a sword.

Mason laying stonework
to face planter walls.

Finished planter walls
with concrete pavers .

Top: Gazebo footing is ready to receive precast concrete structure.

Bottom: Message wall supports classical balustrade.

Right: SHAEF Badge is positioned above Gen. Eisenhower's message to the troops.

Below: Sword Planter is in full bloom.

SCULPTURE

Of the eight scheduled pieces, two were delivered prior to Phase Three and three were to come shortly before the dedication. Six busts of the General Staff were planned to be delivered much later. The "Lady of Trevieres" would be cast by the French government; therefore, the delivery date was not under the direct control of the Memorial designers.

Jim Brothers, lead project sculptor, worked exclusively in his Kansas Studio and personally delivered and supervised the installation of all pieces. His genius brought the Memorial to life.

Jim's Studio

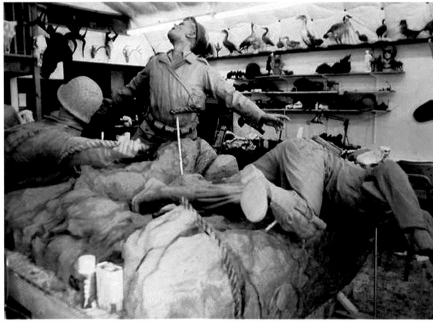

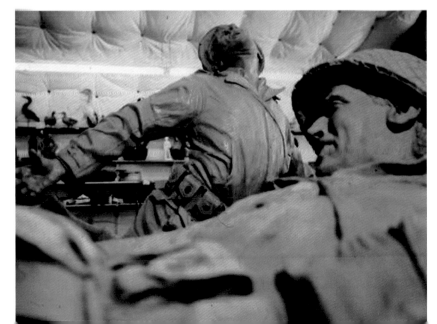

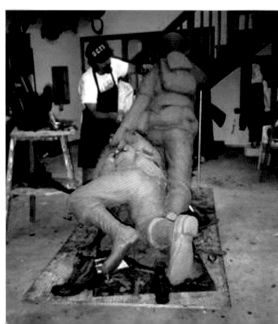

Installation of Beautiful Bronze Statuary

Clockwise from top left:
"Across the Beach" is lowered into place.

"Valor, Fidelity, and Sacrifice" is
positioned in front of Overlord Arch.

Positioning "Through the Surf" with
Jim Brothers supervising.

"Scaling the Wall" is lowered from
Victory Plaza down onto the Storywall.

Over 20,000 guests and dignitaries attended the dedication.

CHAPTER FIVE

Dedication

P resident George W. Bush landed in Roanoke early in the morning of June 6, 2001, and traveled by motorcade from the Regional Airport to Bedford. Thousands were in attendance as the festivities included music, speeches, and a fly-over by Air Force jet fighters. Virginia Gov. James Gilmore introduced President Bush, who in turn, offered a stirring tribute to soldiers and community for raising such a fitting Memorial. For the rest of the day visitors enjoyed full access to the commemorative portion of The National D-Day Memorial.

The President spoke from the bridge.

D-DAY

NATIONAL DEDICATION
JUNE 6, 2001   BEDFORD, VIRGINIA
THE NATIONAL D-DAY MEMORIAL

Clockwise from Top: A veteran recalls the past; President Bush with D-Day veterans; The crowd assembles on Victory Plaza; Many had to wait in the adjoining public areas.

"You have raised a fitting memorial to D-Day, and you have put it in just the right place — not on a battlefield of war, but in a small Virginia town, a place like so many others that were home to the men and women who helped liberate a continent."

Excerpt from President George W. Bush's remarks

(June 6, 2001 at the dedication of The National D-Day Memorial)

Eisenhower Gazebo

CHAPTER SIX

Reality

The story of D-Day began in England. It is, therefore, fitting that a tour of The National D-Day Memorial start in the *English Garden*, move up the hill to *Invasion Plaza*, and ultimately conclude at *Victory Plaza*. As this tour proceeds, the reader is invited to revisit Chapter Three for a discussion of the design inspirations that lead to the creation of the Memorial.

Having previously traced the design and construction from inception to turnkey, this chapter will present a series of images that demonstrate the importance of this Memorial to veterans, their families, and a populace needing to know about the sacrifices made on June 6, 1944.

Main entrance to Victory Plaza

Aerial view of the Memorial Hilltop

Clockwise from top: Inside the Eisenhower Gazebo

Gen. Dwight D. Eisenhower, Supreme Allied Commander

Gen. Omar N. Bradley, commander 12th Army Group,
One of six busts of members of the SHAEF General Staff

From the English Garden a short walk up the Classical Stairs leads to Invasion Plaza.

From Top: Invasion Plaza planter and seating island

After reaching Invasion Plaza an information pylon, typical of many throughout the Memorial, greets visitors.

From Top: Overlord Arch from
the northeast entry gate

Overlord Arch from the
west promenade

West side Necrology Wall where names of the American soldiers, who died during the invasion, are recorded.

From top: East side Necrology Wall records the names of Allied nations' fallen soldiers.

Overall view of Invasion Plaza as seen from Sea Court.

From top: Sea Court looking toward Overlord Arch

Danforth Anchor in Sea Court

Air Court with the L-3B "Grasshopper"

From top: Invasion pool with "Obstacle" and shell burst close by

Invasion pool with obstacle and "Through the Surf" with landing craft beyond

Invasion Pool at dusk

Beachhead Diorama with Storywall in background

From top: "Death on the Shore," "Across the Beach -1"

From top:
"Scaling the Wall"
"Across the Beach"
"Through the Surf"

Top: View looking toward the Bridge over Beach-head and connecting the Air and Sea Courts.

Bottom left to right: The face of combat; A soldier going over the top

From top: "Scaling the Wall" viewed from the bridge looking east.

"Scaling the Wall" soldier hit by enemy fire.

Victory Plaza, Storywall, and Beachhead Diorama from the air

Top: Steps leading up
to Overlord Arch

Left: An isolated view of the
'Peaks of Otter' beyond

Beachhead Diorama and Storywall at night

Top: Pedestrian ramp from Invasion Plaza

Below: Ramp leading up to Victory Plaza

Overlord Arch in Victory Plaza with original model in foreground

Left: "Final Tribute" looking toward the Blue Ridge Mountains.

Bottom left: "Final Tribute" looking toward Bedford, VA

Bottom right: The 'Peaks of Otter' as viewed through Overlord Arch.

Left: Flag Circle with
"Valor, Fidelity, and Sacrifice"
in foreground at
Victory Plaza entrance

Below: The Colleville railing

THE NATIONAL D-DAY MEMORIAL

A gift to the National D-Day Memorial,
the City of Bedford,
and the Nation,
from Guy Wildenstein and his family.
With our eternal gratitude
to the United States of America
for restoring France's freedom,
for granting asylum to our parents,
and for halting the extermination of a people.
In memory
of the American soldiers who gave their lives
on the beaches of Normandy
in June 1944.

Clockwise from top:
The "lady" on the entrance
promenade.

She is a poignant reminder
of the horrors of war.

The "Lady of Trevieres."

From top: Temporary Gift Shop

Gift Shop visitor's deck

Gift Shop veteran's porch

Left: Garrison flag

Below: Main Memorial entrance

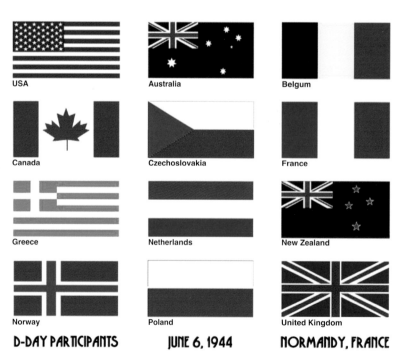

USA

Australia

Belgum

Canada

Czechoslovakia

France

Greece

Netherlands

New Zealand

Norway

Poland

United Kingdom

D-DAY PARTICIPANTS   JUNE 6, 1944   NORMANDY, FRANCE

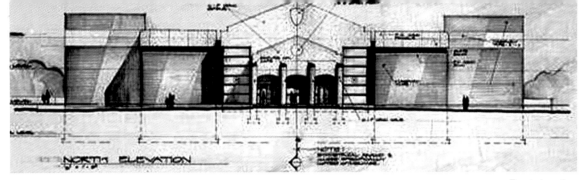

CHAPTER SEVEN

Future

This chapter is not closed. There is still work to be done. Prior to dedication of the commemorative elements, plans were drawn for the construction of an Education Center. These plans were released for bidding and a successful contractor designated to complete the work. However, funds were not available at the time to permit ground breaking for this final and important component of The National D-Day Memorial.

The Education Center will contain 33,000 square feet and provide exhibition galleries, administrative offices, visitor support facilities, archival space, and a theater.

Site plan

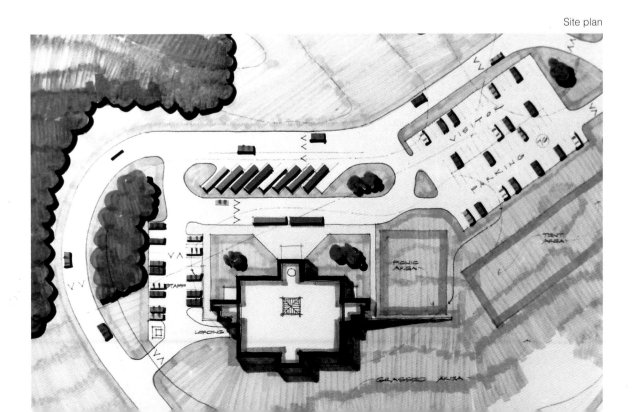

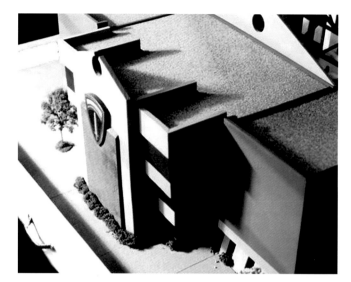

Right: Top view

Below: Rear view overlooking elementary school.

From top: Front view facing Victory Plaza

Entrance enlargement

Left: Grand lobby overlook

Below: Chaplin's Gallery

THE NATIONAL D-DAY MEMORIAL

Top: Schulz Gallery

Left: Mauldin Gallery

Left: Inside Entrance lobby

Below: Entrance lobby looking toward grand staircase.